Animal Babies

created by

BOBBIE KALMAN

art by

GLEN LOATES

BOBBIE KALMAN / GLEN LOATES

Animal Babies

The North American Wildlife Series

CRABTREE PUBLISHING COMPANY

The Glen Loates North American Wildlife Series:
Created by Bobbie Kalman
Art by Glen Loates

Editor-in-Chief:
Bobbie Kalman

Writing team:
Bobbie Kalman
Anne Champagne
Janine Schaub
Moira Daly
Christine Arthurs

Researcher:
Anne Champagne

Editors:

Janine Schaub	Christine Arthurs
Tilly Crawley	Anne Champagne
Moira Daly	Judith Ellis
Louise Petrinec	

Illustrations:
Copyright © 1987 MGL Fine Art Limited.

Photographs:
Page 11: Animals Animals/Leonard LeeRue III
Page 12-13: Animals Animals/Leonard LeeRue III
Page 14: Animals Animals/Z. Leszczynski
Page 15: Animals Animals/C.C. Lockwood
Page 36: Animals Animals/J. Cooke

Design:
Leslie Smart & Associates Limited
Stephen Latimer

Computer layout:
Christine Arthurs

Mechanicals:
Halina Below-Spada   Gerry Lagendyk

Printer:
Bryant Press, with special thanks to Arnie Krause

For Joyce Boucher, with a great deal of admiration

Cataloguing in Publication Data

Kalman, Bobbie, 1947-
    Animal Babies

(The Glen Loates North American wildlife series)
Includes index.
ISBN 0-86505-166-6 (bound) ISBN 0-86505-186-0 (pbk.)

1. Animals - Infancy -Juvenile literature. 2. Mammals - North America - Juvenile literature.   I. Loates, Glen II. Title.   III. Series: Kalman, Bobbie, 1947-   The Glen Loates North American wildlife series.

QL715.K34 1987   j599.03'9'097

350 Fifth Avenue   120 Carlton Street
Suite 3308   Suite 309
New York   Toronto, Ontario
N.Y. 10118   Canada M5A 4K2

Contents

Fuzzy, small, and helpless

What makes babies so special? Is it their tiny size? Is it their big, wide eyes so full of curiosity, or their playful behavior that makes us laugh and feel good about being around them? Perhaps people love babies because these little creatures are helpless. They make us want to protect them.

A brand-new life

A baby, whether human or animal, is a new life. It is a miracle of nature. As it grows, it will explore its surroundings and test its strength. The baby animals in this book are still fuzzy, small, and in need of their parents' care. Parents are a big part of every baby's life. Children often have two parents to care for them. In the case of most animals, it is the mother alone who teaches her offspring about survival. She will make sure that her babies can fend for themselves before she allows them to be on their own. Whereas children stay with their parents for many years, most animal babies grow into adults in just a few months. They have a lot to learn in a short time!

Fun, fun, fun!

All young creatures, including you, enjoy playing and having fun. The animal babies in this book spend many hours each day wrestling, romping, and playing tag with one another. The polar bear cubs on the opposite page enjoy their icy playground. They slip and slide, climb onto snowbanks, and dive into the frigid arctic waters. The small arctic fox below also lives in this cold place. She is taking her very first steps but, before long, she will be romping about playing leapfrog with her brothers and sisters.

In many ways, animal babies are a lot like children. They grow, play, and learn about life. Get to know these fuzzy little creatures and find out just how much they have in common with you!

Mammals just like you

All the baby animals in this book are mammals just like you. Mammals are different from other animals in one special way. Their very first food is their mothers' milk. Only mammal mothers are able to produce milk with which to feed their babies. Besides drinking milk, mammal babies also share many other characteristics.

Born, not hatched

Some animals, such as birds and turtles, lay eggs. Once the eggs are laid, the babies begin developing inside the shells. They hatch when they are ready to meet the outside world. Unlike the babies of these animals, mammal babies develop inside the bodies of their mothers. Mammals give birth to babies that are ready to eat and grow.

Fur and hair

All mammals have fur or hair on their bodies. Some grow an extra-thick coat of fur to keep them warm in the winter, while others need only a thin layer of fur to make them feel comfortable. Human beings do not have fur. We have fine hairs all over our bodies. Because we lack a coat of fur, we must rely on clothes to keep us warm and cozy!

Warm-blooded

Mammals and birds are the only animals that are warm-blooded. If you were to take your temperature for a whole week, you would find that it does not change very much from day to day. This occurs because a mammal's temperature stays the same, no matter what the weather is like outside. Reptiles and other cold-blooded animals do not have regular body temperatures. Their body heat changes with their surroundings. If it is cold outside, their blood gets cold and they cannot move very quickly. The only way cold-blooded animals can warm themselves is by sitting in the sun.

How mammals are born

Mammal babies grow inside their mothers' bodies in a warm and well-protected place called the **uterus**. Inside the uterus a sac filled with a watery liquid, called the **amniotic sac**, cushions and protects the baby as it grows. The baby is attached to its mother by an **umbilical cord**. This cord brings oxygen and nourishment to the baby. At birth an animal mother bites off the umbilical cord, leaving a **navel**, or belly-button, on the outside of the baby's stomach.

Time for the babies!

A mother that is carrying a growing baby inside her uterus is **pregnant**. Some mammals are pregnant for a short period of time, while other pregnancies last much longer. A rabbit may only be pregnant for twenty-six days, but a polar bear is pregnant for eight months. Human mothers carry their babies for nine months.

Each mammal mother finds herself a sheltered place when it is time to give birth. Some babies, such as raccoons, are born blind and helpless. Others, such as the white-tailed deer have young that can walk a few minutes after they are born. All mammal babies, however, need their mother's milk and care to survive.

How many babies?

The group of baby animals born to a mammal at one time is called a **litter**. The size of the litter varies from species to species. Mice give birth to several large litters each year because their young are preyed upon by many other animals. Bobcat babies, on the other hand, are less likely to be killed, so the mother only gives birth to twins. Two healthy kittens per mother are enough to keep the bobcat population constant.

A white-tailed deer licks her nine-minute-old fawn.

At just fifteen minutes after birth, this fawn tries to stand up on its wobbly legs. 13

Nursing

Compared to their parents, newborn mammals are very small. They have a lot of growing to do, so they need to eat often. That is why they always seem to be hungry! The first nourishment mammal babies receive is milk because they cannot digest the solid food that adults eat. The **mammary glands** in a mammal mother's body start producing milk right after the baby is born. The baby nurses immediately by sucking on its mother's nipple.

A mother black bear relaxes with her nursing cubs.

This raccoon mother is snarling at the photographer who has disturbed her while she is nursing her four kits.

The very best milk

Mother's milk is the very best food that babies can have. The milk of each mammal species has nutrients that meet the particular needs of that baby. The milk of the polar bear is rich in fat because polar bear cubs need to develop a layer of fat that will keep them warm in the cold Arctic.

Mammals nurse in different ways. The babies of some mammals, such as the white-tailed deer, can stand almost as soon as they are born. They nurse standing up. The babies suck the nipples on the undersides of their mothers' bellies. Animals whose babies are helpless at birth lie on their sides when they nurse. The babies can reach the nipples without having to move very far. Raccoon babies lie all over their mothers' bellies while nursing. A bat baby nurses by clinging tightly to its mother as she flies through the air.

Solid food

After a few weeks or months mammal babies start eating the same food as their parents do. The mother introduces her babies to this food a little bit at a time. Gradually the young animals eat more and more solid food and drink less milk. This change from drinking milk to eating solid food is called **weaning**.

A job for Mom

Just as your parents look after you, mammal mothers keep their children warm, clean, and properly fed. No other animals care for their young as well as mammals do. As well as giving their youngsters excellent training, mammal mothers also show a great deal of affection and concern for their babies.

Mom the teacher

As a young animal grows, it watches its mother and imitates the things she does. Mothers teach their babies their first important survival lessons. Mammals that are plant-eaters, or **herbivores**, show their young which plants can be eaten and which are poisonous or dangerous. Those that are meat-eaters, or **carnivores**, take their babies on hunting trips. These young animals learn how to hunt by watching their mothers catch food.

Mammal youngsters also find out how to protect themselves from **predators**. Predators are animals that eat other living creatures. Mothers teach their young how to hide and stay very quiet or how to escape if they are chased. Most mothers even risk their lives to defend their babies!

What about Dad?

Not all mammal fathers lend a hand with their offspring. Most leave even before the babies are born. The ones that do stay, however, such as the beaver and the red fox, are a big help to the mothers. They bring food while the mothers nurse their babies. Later on they play an important part in the training of the youngsters.

Leaving home

Mammal babies stay with their mothers until the offspring are ready to face the world on their own. Some stay with their parents for as long as two years. When mammal youngsters become adults, they will also teach their offspring the important lessons of survival.

Beaver kits

Whoosh! Here comes another one! Did you know that baby beavers are born onto their mothers' tails? When the mother is ready to give birth, she sits down with her broad tail placed between her legs. In this position the tail acts as a landing pad catching the young as they are born. Newborn beavers, or kits, are covered in fur, and their eyes are open. They only weigh about half a kilogram each but, by the time they are fully grown, they will weigh as much as an average eight-year-old child.

Everyone back on the tail!

Baby beavers wake up every few hours and cry until they are fed. The mother tucks her tail under her so the new-borns can sit on it to nurse. The kits nurse for about two months. During this time they begin to eat solid food such as tender leaves.

When their little stomachs are full, the kits lie on their backs and yawn. They fall asleep with their paws splayed out in every direction and often start snoring! In a few hours they are hungry again. They wail, fuss, and mutter until their mother feeds them.

Close-knit families

A mother and father beaver stay together their whole lives and share the job of raising their young. Beaver couples are very affectionate, and families are large and close-knit. Kits stay with their parents until they are two years old, so a family usually has a mother, a father, one set of older, and one set of younger kits. This group of ten to twelve beavers is called a **colony**.

These baby beavers are sampling the tender leaves and twigs that they have seen their parents eating.

Water babies

Newborn kits can swim a few hours after birth, but their parents prefer to keep them inside for a couple of months. The kits are so light and fluffy that, if they tried to swim and dive, they would just float on top of the water. A helpless, floating baby might attract a predator, so beaver parents only let their kits leave home after they have put on more weight.

Kits practise swimming by rolling around, doing somersaults, and paddling in circles in the water. When they are first learning to dive, they cannot hold their breath for very long. With practise they are soon able to swim long distances without surfacing. When a kit sees a family member dive, it dives. Older beavers teach younger beavers to slap the water with their tails to signal danger. If a beaver slaps its tail, or hears another beaver tail-slapping, it dives under the water to hide.

Wobbly first home

Beavers build dams to make ponds in which they construct homes called **lodges**. Baby beavers start building at a very young age. Not surprisingly, their first attempts at building dams and lodges produce wobbly and leaky structures. The young beavers, though, are quick learners. Before long their lodges are so strong that even a bear would have difficulty breaking in.

Copy kits

Curious young kits learn a great deal by copying other beavers. If they see their mother nibbling on a juicy poplar or aspen twig, they try it too. Beavers eat other young trees too, as well as grass, ferns, roots, and water plants.

A family construction crew

Building a dam or a lodge involves the entire beaver family.
After an adult has cut down a tree with its sharp teeth, the
whole family, except the youngest kits, helps saw off the
branches. Kits do not have to worry about wearing their
teeth down on rough bark and wood. Beavers are **rodents**.
Their teeth are strong and never stop growing.

Bobcat kittens

How would you like to be born in a cave? You would probably be cold and uncomfortable! But a cave, a covered space between large rocks, or even a hollowed-out log, is the kind of place that a mother bobcat looks for when she is preparing a **den** for her kittens. The kittens need a shelter in which to hide from wolves, coyotes, and other predators. Once a suitable den has been found, the mother bobcat brings plants inside to make the den soft and cozy. Then she is ready to give birth.

It's twins!

In the spring twin bobcats are born. At first they can neither hear nor see. When the kittens are about a week-and-a-half old, their eyes open and their teeth start growing in. Before long they are strong and active. In two months they can climb any tree!

Bobcat kittens are just as full of fun as pet kittens. They stalk, creep along on their bellies, and hide. They jump on their mother and pounce on her endlessly twitching tail. Perhaps pouncing on tails helps in their training as hunters!

Mouse training

The real hunting lessons begin when the mother bobcat brings the kittens their first mouse. At first the kittens just poke at the prey and watch the mouse skitter around. It takes many lessons before they learn to kill and eat their plaything. Once they become experts at mouse hunting, they are able to move on to their main food—rabbit. Bobcats also eat muskrats, foxes, weasels, and other small mammals.

Soon the baby bobcats accompany their mother on hunting trips. Because bobcats are **nocturnal**, they hunt at night and rely on their keen eyesight to spot their prey. The kittens follow their mother by keeping their eyes on the underside of her raised tail and on the white spots on the back of her ears. If one lags behind, its mother calls softly and waves her tail so the kitten can see her!

Bobcat babies are as playful as pet kittens.

Red fox pups

A baby fox is tiny when it is born. It could easily fit into the palm of your hand! A mother fox gives birth to between four and eight small, blind pups in a den. When there is plenty of food, she may have more than ten pups in one litter!

Feeding time

For several days after the baby foxes are born, it is the father's job to bring food to his mate. After the mother has rested, she helps the father with the hunting. She can't stay away too long, though. The pups start whimpering and whining, and these sounds might attract predators. When the mother returns home, she calls softly, and the pups scamper up to the doorway of the den to greet her.

Fox play

Once the pups are out of the den, they spend most of their time playing with one another. They crouch down in the grass and then jump and bite at one another's tails. They chase butterflies and snap at the air. They roll around, race, and even play tag and leapfrog! They are not only having fun; this play helps teach pups hunting and survival skills.

Learning to hunt

Pups nurse for about two months. When their mother thinks that it is time for them to start eating solid food, she lies on her nipples to prevent the youngsters from nursing. Their first solid food is meat that she or the father has **regurgitated**, or spit up. Before too long the mother starts taking the pups on short hunting trips. On the first few trips they jump at beetles and other insects—and usually miss.

Once they have mastered the hunting of insects, Mom drops a mouse in front of them. If they are too slow to pounce, she snaps at them. As time goes on, she places the mice farther and farther away. Soon the pups are eating other small animals, such as rabbits and squirrels. Red foxes also eat nuts and berries.

After the pups are weaned, they need solid food. The search for food is a full-time job for the parent foxes.

This young raccoon has not had much experience catching live food. She wonders how to grab this leopard frog.

Raccoon kits

"Who was that masked animal?" If you hear someone ask this question, you can be certain that the "masked animal" was a raccoon. Raccoons are often called bandits because the dark patches around their eyes make them look as if they are wearing masks. "Bandit" is also a good name for a raccoon because this creature has a habit of raiding garbage cans and stealing food from campsites. Some raccoons are even bold enough to run off with a cake that is cooling on your windowsill. When their stomachs are full, and their faces smeared with icing, they might knock on your window and beg for more!

Raccoons are well known for their ability to solve challenging problems such as unscrewing the lid of a jar or opening a door. The raccoon uses its front paws in almost the same way we use our hands.

Piling on top

A hollow tree is an excellent place for baby raccoons to be born. A mother raccoon nibbles and scratches pieces of wood off the den wall to make a soft bed. Several kits are born in the month of May. The newborns are covered in fuzzy gray fur and cannot hear or see anything until they are three weeks old. They keep warm by piling on top of one another. When the kit on top gets cold, it burrows down into the pile.

While the kits nurse, the mother cuddles them with her front paws. In this position the kits feel warm and happy and usually start to purr. Most kits are weaned by the time they are four months old. After they are weaned, the kits eat frogs, fish, crabs, crayfish, eggs, insects, and various fruits and vegetables.

Watch your step!

Raccoon kits start walking when they are four to six weeks old and can run and climb by about three-and-a-half months. When the kits are still too young to climb down from the den by themselves, it is up to the mother to help them. She picks them up in her mouth and carries them down the tree trunk. Sometimes a kit pokes its head outside the tree den, loses its balance, and falls to the ground. It is usually not hurt—but very surprised! If this happens often, the mother may move her litter to a place closer to the ground.

Family life

Eventually a raccoon family leaves its den and travels around until the fall. Some kits wander away from their mother from time to time, but she always lets them know where she is by twittering to them. When winter comes, the family sleeps together in a new den. A lining of woodchips and leaves makes the den comfortable and cozy. Groups of raccoons who don't belong to the same family sometimes den together to keep one another warm. When spring returns, the kits are old enough to leave their mother.

Frisky kits

Raccoon kits like to play. They race up and down the trunks of trees playing tag or swinging from the branches.

31

Baby gray squirrels

High up in a leafy nest four gray squirrels have just been born. Their eyes are tightly closed and their pinkish skin is loose, wrinkled, and furless. In three weeks the babies will have a beautiful, silky, fur coat.

Did you know that gray squirrels can either be gray or black? The black variety is found mostly in the cold, northern areas of North America. Since dark fur absorbs more of the sun's rays, the absorbed sunlight keeps these squirrels warm. You can see how this works by wearing a dark shirt on a sunny day and then changing into a white one. Which shirt makes you feel warmer?

Loads of energy!

Baby squirrels are full of energy. They run around and around, do somersaults, and take flying leaps. They chase one another and never seem to stay still. Their strong claws help them grip the branches of trees to prevent them from falling off. As they play, they make all kinds of noises. They chatter, bark, and make soft mewing sounds. When they are angry, squirrels sound as if they are muttering nasty things.

"Now, where did I put that nut?"

Young gray squirrels spend a lot of time "squirreling" away food for the winter. Rather than storing great piles of nuts, these squirrels hide one nut at a time in many different spots. Doing this lessens their chances of losing all their stored food. Gray squirrels are very good at finding the nuts they have buried. They have a keen sense of smell and can locate a nut hidden deep beneath the snow.

Baby red squirrels

"Tcher-r-r-r!" scolds the tiny squirrel. "I wanted to explore this hole and there is a woodpecker already in it."

Most animals would probably turn around and run away at the sight of this angry bird, but not the red squirrel! It might stamp its feet, flick its tail, and let the woodpecker know just how annoyed it is!

One or two litters

These peppery little fellows are born in April or May in a hollow tree nest similar to the woodpecker's hole in the picture. To make a comfortable bed for her babies, the mother lines the nest with soft grasses. She usually has one family a year but may raise two litters if she lives in a place where the weather is warm all year round.

The growing season is longer in the south, so a mother may have enough food to feed two litters of squirrels. Just before the babies stop nursing, the mother squirrel moves them to another nest near the edge of her home range. From there the young squirrels can find their own places to live.

High-energy food

Red squirrels live in northern evergreen woods where they can find plenty of pine cones. These tiny animals never seem to stop moving all day, so they need food that provides them with loads of energy. The seeds in pine and spruce cones give them the energy they need.

Red squirrels store their food in secret hiding places throughout the woods. Unlike gray squirrels, which hide their nuts one at a time, the hidden treasures of red squirrels may contain several hundred spruce or pine cones. Some of the buried seeds that the animals have forgotten sprout into trees. You can see how these tiny mammals play an important role in keeping forests full of trees, even if they do not do it on purpose!

Polar bear cubs

It's a good thing that a polar bear can cope with freezing cold weather, for it lives in the far northern part of the world called the Arctic. It is well adapted to this icy place. Not only is it outfitted with a warm fur coat, it also has a thick layer of fat under its skin.

Denning up for the winter

Although adult bears are well protected from the cold, newborn polar bear **cubs** need to be sheltered from the frigid weather. When a female bear knows she is pregnant, she gets down to the serious work of making a comfortable, warm den for her cubs. She hollows out a snowdrift and often makes extra space for a playroom. Arctic blizzards quickly seal up the entrance to the den with snow. The only opening left is a breathing hole that the mother bear makes in the roof.

Cozy and warm

A pregnant polar bear stays in her den for several months. During this time her body temperature drops slightly, and she drifts in and out of sleep. In this drowsy state she gives birth to one or two cubs. The cubs are born blind, deaf, unable to smell, and with almost no fur. There is nothing much for them to do except sleep, nurse, and grow. They snuggle up to their sleepy mother as they drink her warm, rich milk.

Ready to go!

After a month of nursing and snoozing, the baby bears get a bit restless. They test their tiny legs by crawling around the den. Before too long they are climbing all over their playroom and are almost prepared to face the outside world. Their mother is also ready to go outdoors. She has been living off her stores of fat for several months and is hungry for a delicious seal meal!

A mother polar bear gives one of her cubs a lick while it nurses.

The cubs do their best to follow their mother, but their legs wiggle and wobble all over the place, causing the cubs to slip and tumble into her huge footprints. Sometimes the baby bears get so tired that their mother has to piggyback them to a temporary snow cave until they recover.

Built-in sunglasses

When spring arrives, the mother bear and her cubs break out of the den. The great, white world of snow and ice outside is very bright compared to the dark, snug den to which the cubs have been accustomed. Special membranes over the black eyes of the cubs act as sunglasses to keep out the glare of sunshine reflecting off the snow and ice.

Learning by playing

Baby bears learn by playing, watching their mother, and copying what she does. They do somersaults, wrestle, bite, punch, and hug each other. Just as most children love snow and ice, the playful cubs thoroughly enjoy their slippery environment. Their favorite game is sliding down an icy hill on their rumps or bellies, with their legs stretched out as far as they can go. Sometimes their mother catches them at the bottom of the hill.

Swimming lessons

One of the most important things polar bear cubs must learn to do is swim. Swimming is a necessary skill for a lifetime of seal hunting. At the first swimming lesson the mother dunks the cubs underwater once or twice. The cubs float easily because of their thick fur and layer of fat. Sometimes they scamper along the shore and then dive headfirst into the icy water. If they get tired while swimming, they grab onto Mom's tail with their teeth or get a lift on her back.

Fooling seals

Polar bears eat fish, birds, small mammals, and berries, but nothing tastes more delicious to them than a seal! Bears can smell a seal through thick ice and will go to any length to catch it. Sometimes they play tricks to surprise their prey. Bears may pretend to be chunks of ice, covering their black noses with their paws in order to camouflage themselves. As soon as the cubs are ready to walk a fair distance, polar bear mothers take them on seal-hunting trips and teach them the finer points of catching seals!

Time for a swimming lesson!

*The white-tailed fawn magically disappears
into its surroundings.*

White-tailed fawns

This gentle, graceful animal is the baby of the white-tailed deer. It is called a **fawn**. It's mother, a **doe**, has chosen this secluded spot among the soft forest shrubs as the birthplace of her babies. She gave birth to two fawns, but she has hidden one in a different place. If one is found by a predator, the other will still be safe.

The doe returns to nurse the fawns a few times a day. She is careful not to stay with her babies for long, though, because her scent may attract animals that would eat the fawns. Luckily, fawns have almost no scent of their own. They also hide themselves by staying perfectly still. With no scent, sound, or movement, the fawns remain concealed from their predators.

A fawn's spots

Did you notice that this fawn is covered with white spots? These spots look like the bright flecks of sunshine that filter through the trees and shine on the forest floor. They help fawns blend in with the dark-and-light colors of the woods. When the fawn lowers its head, the whole animal magically disappears into its surroundings. By autumn fawns lose their spots and grow their first winter coats. The gray color of their new coats is also good camouflage because it blends in well with the gray-brown winter forest.

Fast runners

Since speed is their best defense, fawns must learn to run early in their lives. They take their first steps just a few minutes after they are born. By the time they are three weeks old, they could easily beat you in a race. The mother brings her offspring together once they can run fast enough to escape danger. Then the two fawns can get to know each other.

Munch, munch; nibble, nibble

After three weeks fawns begin to follow their mother on outings to find food. Although they are still nursing, the fawns munch dandelion leaves or nibble on the tender shoots of small plants. When they are a little older, they eat grass, bark, berries, leaves, and twigs.

Eastern cottontail bunnies

Who would ever guess that an over-grown lawn, an open field, or even a backyard flowerbed could be the secret nesting place of a litter of baby rabbits? The mother cottontail is clever at camouflaging her nest. She burrows out a shallow hole in the ground and makes it soft and cozy with fur pulled from her own belly. She hides the nest with a covering of leaves and grass.

Sometimes two or more rabbit families share the same nest. The rabbits pile one on top of the other and snuggle up for warmth. They often end up in funny positions. One bunny's leg might be propped up against a sister's tummy, while that sister might have her nose pressed against the back of a brother's floppy ear.

"Don't come near my bunnies!"

A mother leaves her young ones alone in the nest during the day while she feeds, but she always stays nearby, just in case. If she finds that another animal has entered her area, she moves the nest to another spot.

Moving the nest is only one way a mother rabbit protects her bunnies. She can be quite fearless when she is guarding her young. She is brave enough to chase away a hawk or fight off a snake that threatens her offspring. When she is forced to fight, her strong back feet come in handy. She leans on her front paws, winds up, and with one powerful "whoop," she can send a small predator flying.

Run and hide

A few weeks after the bunnies are born, the mother rabbit moves her young out of the nest. It is time for them to learn to feed and defend themselves. Their big ears are able to hear the tiniest of sounds. When baby rabbits sense danger, they react in one of two ways: they either stay absolutely still or quickly run away. They double back on their trails, take side trips, or hide in the nearest bush or underground burrow. The predator runs right past them!

Soft thumps and silent sniffs

Rabbits are usually silent creatures. They often communicate with gestures. When they are excited, they stamp their feet. Bunnies make noises only when they are frightened or hungry. A bunny that is really hungry makes little screaming sounds to get its mother's attention. In reply the mother lets out a low grunt. However, when a rabbit is about to be captured, it lets out an ear-piercing cry!

Wildflower salad

After baby rabbits stop nursing, they begin to graze with their mother. They nibble on grasses, wildflowers, bark, and leaves. Clover and alfalfa are their favorite plants, but they also enjoy munching on dandelion greens and ragweed.

Lots of babies

Rabbits grow up quickly. They are on their own within a few months. If a baby rabbit is born in the first litter of the year, it may have babies of its own late that summer. Rabbits are well known for having lots of babies. A mother and father rabbit may have three or four families in one year.

They start a new family as soon as one litter is able to manage on its own. Rabbits must have many babies so they will continue to survive. The forest is full of animals that eat rabbits and, even though thousands are born each year, many do not live to have families of their own.

Mountain goat kids

If mountain goats could understand people, they might wonder why they say such silly things. First of all, people call them "goats," when they are really not goats at all. They are actually related to antelopes!

Are you kidding?

Did you know that female mountain goats are called **nannies** and their babies are called **kids**? Other than the name, however, you and mountain goat kids probably have very little in common. For example, can you imagine being born in a sheltered cranny high in the mountains? Baby goats are! Frisky little goat kids do not waste any time before learning about the world around them. Only minutes after they are born, they struggle to their feet and begin to walk. Before long they have scaled their first steep mountain cliff and are ready to accompany their mother on food-finding trips.

"Now, what do I do?"

Mountain goats have special hoofs that help them climb about in high spots. These hoofs are designed to grip the ground securely with each step. Even with their special feet, however, adventurous baby goats still manage to get into trouble. A mother goat has to watch her frisky offspring carefully to make sure they have grown into safe climbers before she lets them out of her sight. Maybe goat kids and human kids are not so different after all!

Black bear cubs

Did you know that black bears are not always black? The cubs come in a variety of colors, including cinnamon red and sometimes a bluish color. There are even a few black bears that are almost white when they are born!

Playing on their snoozing mother

In winter the female black bear finds herself a cozy den and gives birth to one or two cubs. Like the polar bear she spends the winter in a sleepy state. As the cubs begin to grow, they use their tired mother as a playground. They climb all over her, bite her ears, and roll in her fur. The front legs of baby bears become stronger much more quickly than their back legs do. When the cubs try to walk, their back legs drag behind, so the baby bears often end up moving in circles. The mother bear doesn't mind because this means her cubs can't wander off while she is taking a nap.

Spring awakening

By the time black bear cubs are three months old, their mother is wide awake, and the family is able to leave the den. These are exciting days for the cubs who are anxious to discover their neighborhood. Outside the den they chase butterflies, scurry up trees, sunbathe, and play endless games of tag. But there is danger too. As soon as the cubs venture outdoors, the mother bear teaches them how to climb trees. They learn to recognize the mother's "woof-woof," which means, "Climb a tree right now—there is danger nearby!" When the coast is clear, she makes a whimpering sound, and the cubs shimmy back down, rear end first.

When looking for food, baby bears depend on their senses of smell and hearing more than their sight. They search for berries, roots, honey, and nuts. Although they eat mostly plants, black bears also eat a few small animals, insects, and fish.

After the cubs leave the den, they explore the neighborhood in search of food. These lucky cubs have found a delicious honey snack. Besides honey, black bears eat the bees as well!

Mammal homes

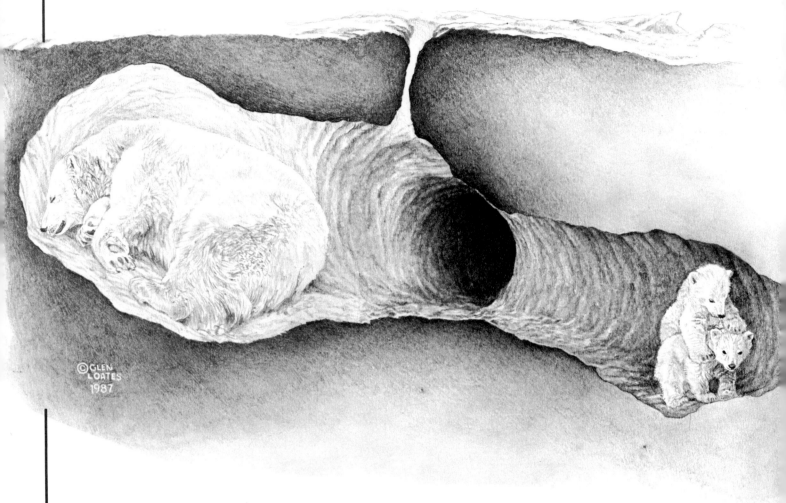

Although mammals are the most highly developed animals, they make the simplest homes. They use these homes to give birth but generally do not return to them after the young have left the nest. Any covered spot, from a hollow log to a cave, makes a satisfactory home for many mammals. Some mammals dig burrows under the ground. When the white-tailed deer is preparing to give birth to her fawns, she simply settles in a safe patch of greenery.

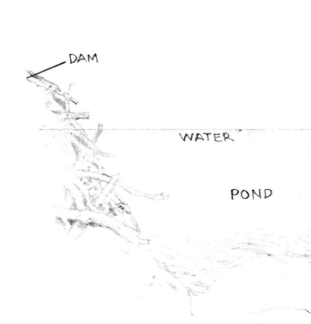

DAM

RES
ELE

WATER

POND

Polar bear dens

Polar bears dig their dens out of a snowdrift rather than out of the ground. In November or December a pregnant female tunnels down and makes two spaces—one for herself and another as a playroom for her cubs. The mother and her cubs stay in their den for nearly six months. When spring arrives and the light starts filtering in through the ceiling of the den, the mother breaks through the roof and the cubs get their first peek at the outside world.

Beaver lodges

The beaver is one of the best builders in the animal world. It lives in a pond that it has made by building a dam across a stream. The dam is a combination of logs, roots, and whatever else happens to be around. It is filled in with mud and often contains small stones. Some dams are four meters high and longer than a football field!

Once the river is dammed, a deep pool forms behind the dam. The beaver builds its lodge somewhere near the middle of the pond. Inside there are often separate rooms, each with a dry floor raised above the water level. The entrances to the lodge are underwater, so predators can't get in.

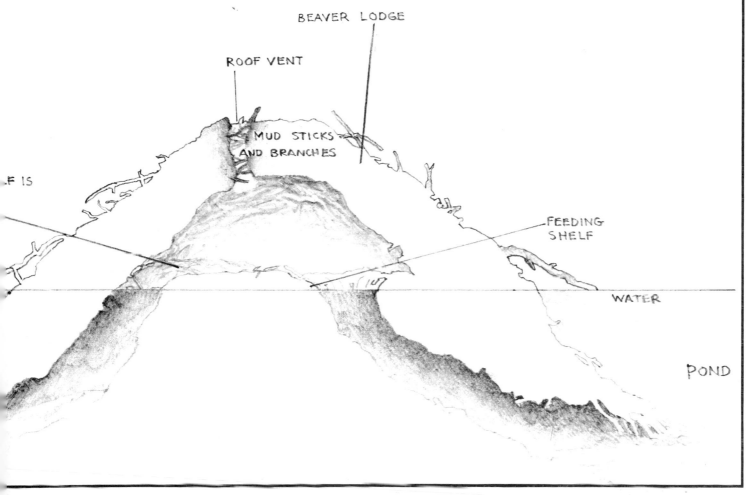

BEAVER LODGE

ROOF VENT

MUD STICKS AND BRANCHES

F IS

FEEDING SHELF

WATER

POND

What's special about ...

mountain goat hoofs?

Have you ever wondered how mountain goats could live on such high cliffs without slipping off? It's easy! They can do this because they have specially adapted feet for climbing. The leathery underpads on their soles cushion their hoofs and provide the goats with traction, helping them stand more securely. These underpads also protect the hoofs from rough surfaces.

Mountain goat hoofs are split in two like pliers. The goats can spread their toes and then close them tightly around the edge of a rock. Mountain goats are able to walk on cliff ledges that are as narrow as five centimeters!

beaver teeth?

How would you cut down a tree? If you were a beaver, you would use your teeth! Beavers are rodents and, like all rodents, their large upper and lower teeth never stop growing. They constantly wear down their teeth by gnawing on trees. They also grind their teeth together to keep them sharp. If a beaver is sick or unable to gnaw, its teeth still continue to grow. Teeth that are not worn down can get so long that they curve back into the poor beaver's jaw and may eventually kill it.

squirrel tails?

When young squirrels leap from branch to branch, they don't always land where they want to! If one of these eager jumpers misses its landing spot, its thick, bushy tail fans out and works like a parachute! As the squirrel falls, air rushes through its tail, slowing it down so that the little animal rarely injures itself when it lands.

A squirrel tail does more than just act as a parachute. A big, fluffy tail makes a great blanket for a cold evening. It can also be a wonderful parasol. A squirrel often lies on a branch with its tail flung over its back for shade. When swimming, the tail steers the squirrel along, and when it is leaping from branch to branch, the tail helps it keep its balance. The tail is even used to communicate. There is nothing like the flick of a tail to let one squirrel know that another is mad!

polar bear paws?

Polar bears may be small and playful when they are born but, by the time they are fully grown, their bodies are huge and powerful. Did you know that the paw of an adult polar bear weighs as much as a six-or seven-year-old child? This great paw is so dangerous that it can easily rip an animal to pieces. With one mighty swat the polar bear can break in the roof of a seal's icy den or even kill a seal!

Activities

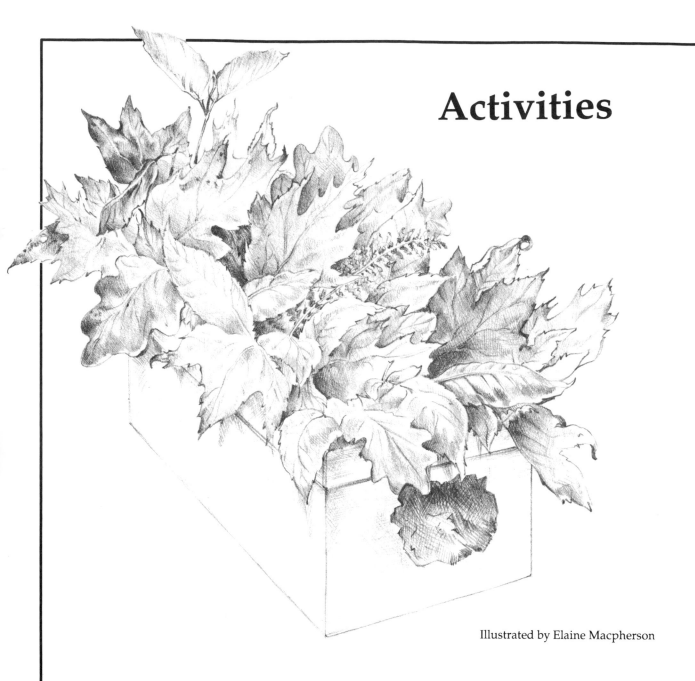

Illustrated by Elaine Macpherson

Make a squirrel dray

A squirrel's nest, also called a dray, can be found high in the tops of trees. A dray is covered with leaves and sticks. Inside, the hollow interior is covered with soft grasses, fur, and moss. You can make your own model dray by using a shoe box with a hole cut in one end for the entrance. Collect leaves and twigs and cover the outside of the box with them. Decorate the inside of your squirrel's dray with soft materials found in and around your home. You might want to use shredded newspaper, cotton balls, bits of material, or even hair from your hairbrush! After you've finished your dray, you can set it outside and see if any squirrels move in! Instead of a realistic dray, you might decide to make an imaginary squirrel house. Decorate the inside with a leaf hammock, acorn dishes, and firefly light fixtures!

Tail-slapping, hand-clapping talk

If you were a beaver, you would slap your tail on the water to signal another beaver. Let us suppose that one slap meant "Danger!" What might two and three slaps mean in beaver language? Make up a list of beaver signals and write down what you think each signal means.

Since you have no tail to slap on water, you may want to clap your hands to communicate in beaver language. You can vary your claps by making them long, short, loud, and soft. Make up a hand-clapping code for the words "fun, play, hide, run," and teach the codes to your friends. When you speak, replace these words with your code claps and see if your friends understand your message.

Baby buttons

After reading this book, you will have learned many new and interesting facts about baby animals. You may have even done some extra work on your own to find out more about one particular animal. It is a shame to keep all this knowledge to yourself! Make a button that says, "Ask me about animal babies," and pin it on your shirt. When your friends ask what your button means, you will be able to tell them some fascinating animal facts!

A baby bobcat

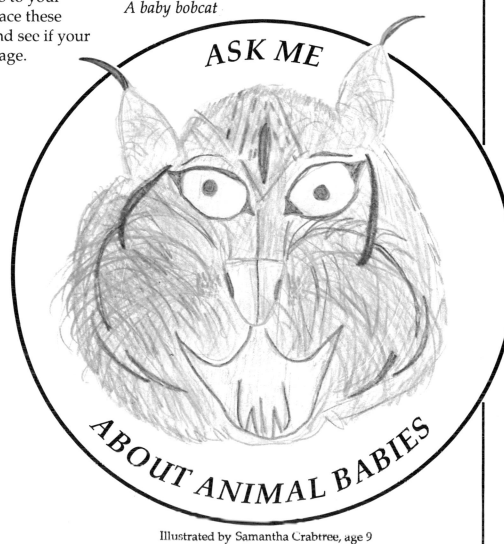

Illustrated by Samantha Crabtree, age 9

Glen with his sons Christopher and Michael.

Glen Loates

Ever since Glen Loates was a child, his love of animals has led him to try capturing our natural world in drawings, paintings, and sculpture. As a boy he spent as much time as he could exploring neighborhood streams and woods. He started sketching interesting scenes during hikes and used these sketches to do more detailed illustrations.

Now, as a professional artist, Glen works in a light-filled studio in his own home. He has a natural history library and often borrows materials, such as animal pelts, from museums to help him make his paintings as realistic as possible. Glen also uses wildlife video tapes, clippings, and photographs from nature magazines as reference material for his work. Yet, no matter how much time Glen spends in the studio, he still thinks of the wilderness as his real working space.

A word from Glen

When I was a young boy just learning to draw, I was frustrated because I could not make my pictures realistic enough. Before long, though, I found out that I could greatly improve my sketches by doing them over and over. I took time to sketch every single day and, as if by by magic, my hands began to draw what my eyes were seeing.

If you are a budding nature artist, the best thing you can do is to draw as much as possible. Keep a daily sketchbook and hold onto both your good and bad drawings because they will help you see just how much your work has improved. If you start a collection of photographs and magazine clippings, you will have plenty of reference material to help you with your practise sketching—but don't just work with other people's pictures. Take as many field trips as possible and create your own impressions of nature.

Cottontail bunny sketches

Over the years Glen has had many families of rabbits make nests in the long grasses of his back yard. He has had the opportunity to watch these furry neighbors both through binoculars and up close. When Glen discovers a cottontail nest on the ground, he never disturbs the baby bunnies as he observes them squiggling around.

These are quick sketches of cottontail bunnies. Notice how Glen has detailed the eyes. Glen always draws the eyes of animals first.

Glossary

adapted - Having made changes to fit situations or surroundings.

alfalfa - A plant with purple flowers and green clover-like leaves.

bond - A special closeness.

burrow - The hole or tunnel dug by a small animal, such as a rabbit or a mole.

burrow - To dig a hole or tunnel.

camouflage - To change the look or actions of something in order to disguise it.

cranny - A small, narrow opening like a crack.

den - A wild animal's home or retreat.

doe - A female deer or rabbit.

evergreen (tree) - A tree that has green leaves or needles the entire year.

fawn - A deer that is less than a year old.

fleck - A small patch of light or color.

graze - To eat growing plants.

litter - A group of animals born at one time to one mammal mother.

mammary gland - The organ in a female mammal that produces milk.

membranes - Thin layers of tissue that cover a part of the body or body surface.

nanny - A female goat.

nourishment - The nutrients found in food that living beings need to stay healthy.

nutrient - A food substance that a living being needs to be healthy and strong.

parasol - A small, light umbrella.

peppery - Hot-tempered.

pine - An evergreen tree that grows cones and has needle-shaped leaves.

predator - An animal that eats other animals.

prey - An animal that is hunted and eaten by another animal.

reptile - A cold-blooded animal that has a spine and dry, scaly skin. Snakes and lizards are reptiles.

scent - An animal's odor that distinguishes it from other animals.

species - A distinct animal or plant group that shares similar characteristics and can produce offspring within its group.

twitter - A light, chirping noise.

underpad - The soft cushioning under the toes of an animal protecting its feet from rough surfaces.

uterus - The organ in a female mammal that holds and nourishes a baby until it is born.

wean - To teach a baby to eat foods other than its mother's milk.

Index

3456789 BP Printed in Canada

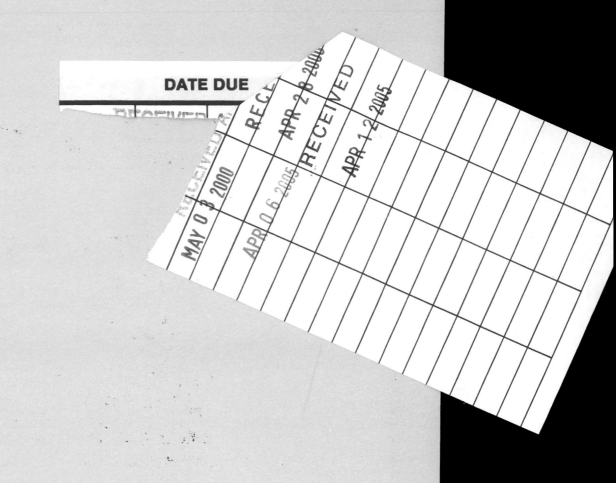

Index

3456789 BP Printed in Canada